# Love Tides...
## and Golden Isles Lore

~Anna Gitana Layton~

# Love Tides...
## and Golden Isles Lore

**Terry Herbert**

*Terry Herbert*

*B*House ™
*B*House Publishing
Brunswick, Ga. 31523

## Terry Herbert

Copyright © 2002 By: Terry Herbert
Post Office Box 24588
St. Simons Island, Ga.31522

ISBN  0-9653831-2-1

**Published By:**

*B*House Publishing Co.
716 Fancy Bluff Road
Brunswick, Georgia 31523
E-Mail:  bhouse@darientel.net
(912) 265-2490
(912) 264-0660

# Contents

## *Part II*
## Love Tides In!

**<u>Part III</u> – Love Tides Out!**  *(con't)*

# <u>Art Credits</u>

## Anna "Gitana" Layton

Pages: Cover, 26,27,56,98,106,
107,113

## Heather A. Eades

Pages: 28,30,32,40,42,44,50,
58,64,72,76,82,84,86,108,118

## Julee Crews

Pages: 34,38,63

Page Layouts & Design
LaRon D. Bennett, Sr.

## Dedication

This Book is dedicated to my twin sons, Geoffrey and Christopher, who, although too young to appreciate it now, may find it helpful in dealing with Love Tides in the future. My dear boys have a writing gift also. Maybe they will dedicate a book to me sometime!

# Foreword

In 1606, William Shakespeare wrote the romantic comedy, "Twelfth Night." The play featured the famous line, "If music be the food of love... play on." At this same time, coastal Georgia was entering a relative period of peace led by Franciscan missions after years of bitter warring between Timucuan and Guale Indians and rival Spanish military forces. These remnant tribes of local Native Americans, enjoyed and respected life in this scenic area. Mounds of oyster shells can still be seen today on St. Simons, where farmers held huge oyster roasts.

St. Simons Island is a lovely resort community, nestled between salt marshes and the Atlantic Ocean just off the southeastern tip of Georgia. Nearby Jekyll Island and Sea Island are also popular destinations. The fourth Golden Isle is Little St. Simons Island which offers limited access and accommodations, but unspoiled beauty. This area is noted all over the world for its beautiful beaches, massive stands of moss-draped oaks and pines, good food and friendly residents. It also boasts a rich history, going back to the prehistoric Native Americans who lived on the islands several thousand years ago. In 1736 St. Simons Island became a southern outpost in Oglethorpe's line of defense around Savannah, Georgia.

St. Simons is also home to historic Christ Church, one of the oldest preaching sites on the Atlantic Seaboard. Because of its abundant wildlife, this area of Coastal Georgia is a paradise for nature lovers of all ages. The passageway to these islands is the charming and historic city of Brunswick.

Terry Herbert moved to St. Simons Island from Athens, Georgia, in July of 2000. He is a tour guide, history buff, teller of local stories, and is a prolific writer of classical romantic poetry. Since moving to St. Simons Island in July 2000, Terry has compiled scores of romantic poems set in Coastal Georgia. "Quill Publications," "The Brunswick News" and the "Golden Isles Weekend" newspaper have published his poems. The Cloister, where he made regular appearances in spring of 2001, was first to nickname him, "The Golden Isles Poet." He has also performed at the Jekyll Island Club Hotel, local art associations, and the Three Rivers Regional Library. At local schools he has told stories, presented his own poetry and introduced the works of William Shakespeare. Terry's work boasts an uncanny insight into the human condition and the various ways people perceive and relate to each other.

If you have just fallen in love, there is something here for you and your partner. If you have been together for a very long time, there is something here for you and your mate. If you are lonely and feeling a bit down, you'll find hope and support in these lines. Only love can energize our emotions to laugh, to cry, to sigh, and to feel on such a profound level. Now it's your turn. Come along, as this book of poetry and art explores the Golden Isles.

Jim Pettigrew
Author, "The Business of Music Marketing and Promotion," Billboard Books

# Acknowledgements

Special thanks to God, and to my 13-year-old identical twin sons, Geoffrey and Christopher, for getting me through a process and this project.

I am profoundly grateful to Jim Pettigrew for his encouragement in seeing this manuscript's potential, for arranging a meeting with the publisher, and for writing the Foreword. I am forever indebted to Anna "Gitana" Layton who just happened to be passing through the Golden Isles just when our attention was turning to the cover of the book and the illustration of several key poems. (Her planned two weeks on Jekyll Island lasted six months). Also, thanks to my second cousin, Heather A. Eades, for a year's worth of good art, as well as Julee Crews, a talented local artist.

Thanks to Charlotte Harrell for her artistic insights into both writing and art and to The Island Players' icon and director, Joan Harris, for coaching my delivery; Karen Snell for historical research; Sean Luke, and Susan Spessard, my cousin and a French teacher for help on French. Special thanks to Keith Johnson, my theater brother from the "Town And Gown" performances of "Much Ado About Nothing" Athens, GA. for co-writing a poem, Mary Wishart, editing and St. Simons Library for "hundreds" of hours on their computer. (They say if this book sells well, I owe them a new one!)

Thanks to my first friends on St. Simons Island during my week of vacation, Jeanne Greenberg and Kellie Parr. Thank you to ladies who provided inspirations: Tracy Conner, Deborah Willoughby, Susan Chastain, Marian Reudlinger, Joyce Yeattes, Heather Pruitt, Tannis Allen, Kirby Powers, Heather Marshall, Deborah Blunt, Sandra Strickland, Beth Downey and Caroline Butler. Several of those became advisors as well as Sue Anderson, Jane Miller, Cary Knapp and Bill Tipton. Thanks to the Jekyll Island Art Association for scheduling my first presentation of my new poetry, The Cloister, for a number of opportunities to share with their guests, as well as the new Sea Island Golf Lodge. Thanks to the students at St. Simons Elementary, Oglethorpe Point Elementary, Frederica Academy, and Risley Middle School for responding enthusiastically to my poetry, stories and introduction classes to Shakespeare. Finally, thanks for opportunities to speak to Elderhostels, and for the opportunity to be the guest of Little St. Simons Island for a day!

# Preface

## Art Makes That Pleasant To Contemplate Which Would Be Painful To Experience

When Terry Herbert walked up to my display of paintings at a July, 2000 exhibit, he started quoting entire sonnets by William Shakespeare. To me, this stranger had one thing in common with that poet–he lacked a biography. So when he moved from quoting Shakespeare's love poems to quoting his own, I felt uneasy. He was talking about romance, about feminine beauty, and yes, even about the moon, the tides, and summer nights. That way, I thought, lies risks of the heart, risks of truth, and even worse, risks of cliché.

Yet, as I listened to more of them, I could see why they were appealing. They were expressions of response to female beauty that has nearly disappeared. The whole vocabulary of innocent rapture—man to woman, woman to man–has been deemed suspect the precursor to some "sell," or worse,"sell–out." In its place have come song lyrics to crude to deserve a name and daily speech too starved to inform the speaker, much less the listener.

One day this emerging poet and I spoke of scripture. I said that of two kinds of love–the one committed, supported by God, and the other romantic, wrenching the emotions, I would take the former. Then Terry recited his poems to me; they used images of the sea to venture into heartbreak and loss, and back out of it into a redeemed experience of life. When he feels at the limits of his inspiration, he goes back to Shakespeare. For close observation, he likes,"that time of year thou mayst in me behold when yellow leaves or none, or few, do hang upon the boughs." When Shakespeare ends his metaphor of age as snuffing out life the way ashes snuff out flame on a log: a flame consumed with that which it was nourished by, his graceful words have tamed a grim subject.

Terry Herbert thinks poetry can console and heal. He likes the words of Austin Warren: "art makes that pleasant to contemplate, which would be painful to experience, or even, in life, to witness."

Herbert's poems voice the adoring response of the boy's heart in the man. Although it takes a grownup to turn that into love, it is sad to push out of a man's consciousness the words for the charm he finds in women, and in commitment to love. Terry Herbert found the voice of love's response in the sand and sea of the Golden Isles of Georgia. He even wants our coastal charm known for this power, and he has the poems to prove it.

Charlotte Harrell

# Introduction

"I'll give you a chance if you move me to St. Simons." These words from a wife who had been threatening divorce, offered the opportunity I had long been waiting for! I had written a poem earlier that week of vacation which had led, one day later, to an invitation for me to share my poems at a meeting in The Village. This half–hour presentation, mostly from memory, had resulted in an offer from a popular island band for me to write lyrics for them. The words for two songs followed on the vacation's last two days. What a vacation!! And now this...

I had written six romantic poems in the sixteen months before that vacation week. The deep emotion behind these inspirations was the realization that I could lose my love of over two decades. But, along with the potential loss, came the emergence of a gift of romantic poetry which I never possessed before. Between the first poem, "Yours Is The Beauty," in February of 1999, and the next, "What Lies Beneath The Snow," in November of that year, I had begun to immerse myself in the memorization of sonnets, songs, and excerpts from the writings of William Shakespeare. I continued this mild "obsession" through spring of 2000 when I auditioned for and landed a role in "Much Ado About Nothing" with the "Town and Gown Theatre" of Athens, Georgia. I initiated this cultured discipline as a means to win back my love after she brought home books about Shakespeare from the library and wanted to study them. My approach seemed to be working the first month, but later became just one more source of irritation to her.

This brings us to my life-changing vacation week at St. Simons Island in June of 2000. I found this "artsy" island, the home of Eugena Price and her popular historical fiction, to be a place where my poetry could get more of a reaction than I was receiving in my rural county, "Aint that Purty!" I moved to St. Simons one month later, with my eleven-year-old twins Geoffrey and Christopher, following me after three weeks. But I was not prepared for the magnitude and frequency with which inspiration was to come in this charming island and coastal area. I peered out into the pre-dusk ocean my first day here and the sea beckoned me to write "On Maids and the Ocean." Two days later, "On Men and the Sea" followed. For the next four months, the Golden Isles "mused" and amused me with a new poem every four days on the average. And this despite the preoccupation of playing the role of "Mr. Brownlow" in the Island Players' production of the musical, "Oliver." I was Oliver Twist's grandfather and my twins were cast as workhouse orphans and pickpockets during the three week long performances on St. Simons Island.

Two weeks after my move, I visited Jekyll Island for the first time ever and was hired to give narrated tours of the Historic District. I had been a historical tour guide in Athens, but the new medium of transportation was horse drawn carriages pulled by beautiful draft horses. In addition to the leisurely tour of the million-aire cottages and clubhouse, by night I often recited poetry to loving couples on romantic, moonlit carriage rides. The lore of that island also captured my heart and inspired more poetry.

I have also enjoyed serving as a first mate on dolphin tours as well as an historical tour guide on St. Simons Island. Through invitations to speak at The Cloister, I became familiar with Sea Island's world-wide appeal. The last of the Golden Isles I was privileged to visit was Little St. Simons Island. It wasn't just another island, it was another world! Sitting on the lap of Brunswick's 900 year-old "Lover's Oak" was another unique experience as I felt and wrote into poetry the story the ancient tree seemed to want me to tell.

During September, 2000, my questions were changing from an optimistic, "When is my love coming?," to "Is she coming at all?" to finally, "If she doesn't come, will I find a new life without her?" As grim realities set in, my despair was diminished as I began to make friends with some of the island's and coastal Georgia's ladies. Eventually, I would have an occasional walking and workout partner, a regular jogging partner, a prayer partner, a ballroom dance partner through the Focus singles group, and finally, a special visitor to the Golden Isles, who became a long distance friend and confidant. They all became my good friends, and they are all beautiful ladies in their youthful 30's to early 40's.

"Love Tides and Golden Isles Lore" is a book of cresting waves of inspiration which struck this newcomer, as I was befriended by residents and even visitors, plus the beauty and the lore of these breath-taking and breath-giving islands. As I penned the opening verse about the Jekyll Island Club's eccentric original member, McEvers Bayard Brown, who never recovered from being jilted by his fiancée, I realized I was confronting my own options:

"A port though a haven between land and the sea,
Becomes a portal for adventure's liberty
From land's disillusionment and lost love's misery.
Could it become a chain from which you cannot break free?"

# Golden Isles Lore

# The Lady of the Tide

While white foamed crests crash the rocky shore,
The tide comes in, the tide comes in,
Our playground's now an ocean floor!
Sun bathers, swimmers, fishermen,
Retrieve their things and rush inside.
They all have left, they all have left,
But the Lady of the Tide!

While she stands upon the seashore,
A calm amidst wild waves.
The tide comes in, the tide comes in,
And, yet, by her the sea behaves!
The water's flowing, her brown hair blowing,
Features of youth and beauty abide!
Of land and sea, o come to me!
O Lady of the Tide!

The land is land, the sea is sea,
Yet oft at tide the two do meet.
When tide comes in, when tide comes in,
They kiss, then clash by lunar beat.
St. Simons lore must add one more,
Two forces of nature defied!
For land and sea revealed to me
The Lady of the Tide!

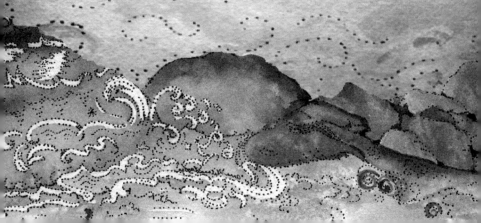

# On Maids and the Ocean

Ocean, you are not one to fickle share
  Like many maids of face and body fair,
    For they in fanciful whims may come and go.
    Yet, despite your oft tides of high and low,
      Still, men may chart your course and
        moody swings,
        While I know not what changes a day brings.
    In love with the lady I cherish most,
      O men, in vain we woo them and we boast!
    Loves which flourish long ere ending in tears
    Still cannot be measured in Ocean years.
  So, dear Sea, I lean on you and your flows,
  In love, I do no more than just suppose.

# On Men and the Sea

Thousands of ripples fill my late day Ocean view.
Whenever did scenery teem with so much life?
Each few seconds, the waves try to do something new.
Therapy, they are, for those seeking haven from strife.
Sea, I, too, kneel humbly before your majesty.
My pressured life I bring and lay at your altar.
In doing so, my spirit wells up within me
And determines, no, never again to falter!

Sea, locked in you is the wisdom of the ages—
So unshackled, unfettered, unbounded and free!
Being near you turns back my mind to the sages,
Where I find explanation for your liberty.
For you bow to no man's office, business or fame.
You flow thousands of miles from the lands of men.
You refuse to be captured, contained or renamed.
The Sea is its own captain and shall be ev'n when
The continents no longer are occupied by men!!

## Six Months At Sea

Six Months On An Island, She Looks Out To Sea.

Six Months Being An Island, Emotionally.

Their Love Goes Back To High School Days As Sweethearts.

They Married, The Navy And Sea Split Them In Parts.

There Are Many Years In Six Months Of Waiting,

There Are Many Tears In Time Barely Abating.

Six Months At Sea Seems Like An Eternity!

He Gazes Toward The Shore, She Looks Out To Sea.

They Are True Lovers Who Yearn, Two Lovers Who Burn,

Who Live For The Chance A Calendar Page To Turn!

At Last, When Separation Is Numbered In Days,

The Navy Finds Reasons To Call For Delays.

Then, Heather Longingly Wants To Stay On The Beach,

While Hal's Still Encouraged She's Almost Within Reach.

In Days Past The Ship Would Appear At The Port,

Though Now, Reunions Are Of A Different Sort.

But The Ending's The Same, Pent-up Feelings Displayed,

They Run, Embrace, Make Memories Never To Fade!

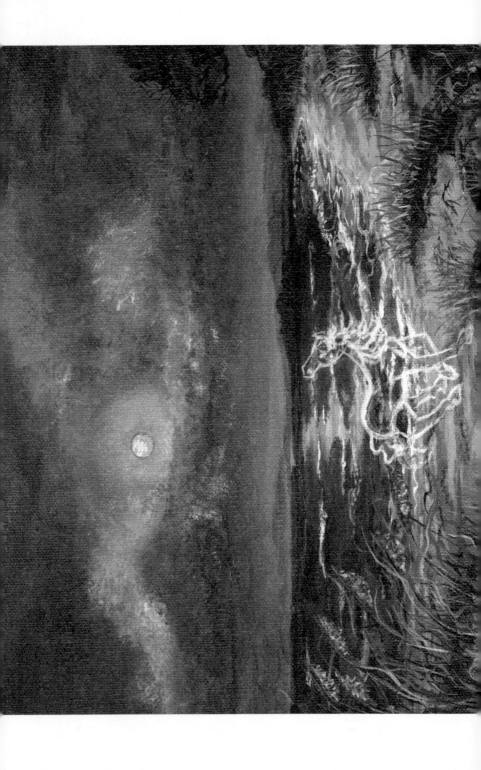

# The White Horse of Jekyll

The resounding, pounding hoofs of the White Horse of Jekyll,
At night, may strike up a beat along the "Marshes of Glynn."
It's form is like a mist, its shape the White Horse of Jekyll –
A ghostly, ghastly sight even without the hoof beats din!!

This phantom has galloped for centuries, the White Horse of Jekyll,
A stallion left by the Spanish, that learned to live as wild.
In time forgot the scent of man, this White Horse of Jekyll,
And for some years, the island was a wilderness undefiled.

But then a ship with men was glimpsed by the White Horse of Jekyll,
He snorted, turned and galloped, eluding the men for a while.
But they sought to make him their prize, the White Horse of Jekyll,
His heart was large but he lived on the smallest Golden Isle.

A cavalryman landed to capture, the White Horse of Jekyll,
Twelve Horsemen, and bloodhounds pursued until the white beauty tired.
His hoofs could have crushed dogs and men, the White Horse of Jekyll,
But he raced to a bluff, gazed seaward, and there he seemed inspired.

He galloped right off the bluff, the White Horse of Jekyll!
A piercing, frightened scream accompanied his leap to be free!
As he plunged downward into the waves, the White Horse of Jekyll,
The men glimpsed his head and mane, then he... sank to the bottom of the sea!!

And that's why he is heard even now, the White Horse of Jekyll,
Resounding, pounding hoofs in the wood, sand dunes and the beach!
There have even been sightings on waves, the White Horse of Jekyll!
And who can capture him now? A phantom dwells beyond reach!!

# Lover's Oak

An Oak almost as old as love
Adorns a Brunswick neighborhood,
A canopy of branches spread above
Nine hundred years of gnarled wood.

It's known by the name of Lover's Oak,
Where, once, Indian braves met their maidens.
Here they loved, slept and then awoke,
Beneath great branches, magic laden.

What tree could possess such mystery?
The Spanish moss like fairy dust,
In moonlight, illuminates the tree
From its girth to its outer thrust.

And Lover's Oak may even have a heart,
That beats when lovers embrace below,
And quiets when lovers quarrel and part.
This Oak makes friends, but never a foe.

It was so centuries ago,
An Indian princess came here to meet
Her warrior lover with his bow.
The tree's massive lap became their seat.

And I would not be surprised to learn
That each knob along the tree's rough bark,

## Lover's Oak (con't)

Is there to mark couples who return,
Whose love lasts decades past that first spark!

Much more may be learned from Lover's Oak,
Our love must stay "green" through whole years,
A resource of strength which we invoke,
With roots as vital as what appears,

A life strong to endure endless storms,
A hide as tough as this Oak's bark.
For scars and gnarls its character warms,
Remembering day, when all is dark.

Is Lover's Oak really one or two?
A center so joined cannot sever
In a union both old and new!
So must lovers who love forever!

For passion's flames blaze full, then diminished,
Much like the limb's resurrection fern.
Just when we think that it is finished,
One shower invites life to return!

The branches reach high, yet down to man.
So must my limbs reach up toward God!
That He may finish what He began,
For we, like this Live Oak, come from sod.

# St. Simons Island's Distinction

St. Simons holds a subtle distinction,
Of good ol' qualities fighting extinction.
Although developers have made their mark,
The feel of the island's much like a park.
The oaks still flourish from "The Lighthouse" view,
Accenting the old while hiding the new.
While sea gulls glimpsing beach houses on shore,
May notice that there seem to be more,
The ocean breezes could be sighs of relief,
That building of hotels seems to be brief.
As beaches are not overly crowded.
Cottages are not dwarfed or enshrouded.

It never takes long for islanders to show
Their guests a villiage like those long ago.
The Villiage where shopping is a delight,
And restaurants please diners day or night.
A place where one can go at day's end
And count on finding at least one good friend.
For those who would rather serve their own dish
The Pier is so handy, where they can fish.
While watching for their bobber and line to dip,
They may admire a huge passing ship.
And usually the backdrop is blue sky,
With white cotton clouds that don't seem that high.

And if by this time you feel totally inspired,
Then go to Christ Church, learn what has transpired,
Beginnings of the island or of the world
Revealed on stain glass, in pictures unfurled!!

41

## A Bride And Widow On One Day

It's rare one day's joys and sorrows do thus converge.
When, else, did a wedding end with a funeral dirge?
A white bridal gown changed to a widow's black dress,
And plans for her happiness to end in distress!
Her two men contrast - one, the man she loved, her groom,
The other, a former suitor, a cloud of doom!
Her past and present collided with one fatal shot!
A bride and widow on one day, became her lot!

A beautiful woman can drive men to desperation,
And Francis Fannie Schlatter was quite an attraction!
Her dark hair and her eyes, who could resist!
Her suitors were lined up determined to persist.
She chose Eardley Westmoreland her husband to be,
But, he was shot and killed after the ceremony!
Her hopes, her dreams perished - an act of senseless rage!
Before loving once again, nine years she would age.

Now, time is an ally to the most troubled soul.
The years of sighing, crying, trying, made her whole!
For Fannie Schlatter Westmoreland would, again, wed,
And John Eugene du Bignon was where her heart was led.
A most influential figure of Jekyll Island,
The man who sold Jekyll, became her new husband.
To them was born a daughter with a striking "flaw,"
For she, too, was so pretty, she kept men in awe!

43

## Children, the Elderly and the Sea

How the eyes of a child see from a different perspective!
Ceilings are miles above their heads, the room irrespective.
Living in a world of giants and chairs awfully high,
When overcome by these challenges, they all the harder try!
Yet I know a place where child and adults are equalized.
I know a place where gaps between young and old are minimized.
Where the sky is as high to grown-ups as to a child.
Where the ocean stretches for endless miles, peaceful or wild.
Where the man of one hundred feels like the child of ten!
Where the woman of ninety feels like she can't remember when
She ever felt closer to the ocean's watery throne,
Where small differences in children and the elderly are shown!
Where distinctions like sandcastles are leveled at high tide,
Leaving, in its wake, brand new beaches that are level and wide.

# The Name of Tannis

It  is amazing how ladies can make any name beautiful!
Names, by themselves, not associated with beauty's high  graces,
Fall to the mundane and unfairly dwell as though unsuitable.
But place the name, Tannis, on one of God's most beautiful faces,
It sprouts wings and soars like a goddess of Greek mythology,
It glitters like a westward island's sunset, exhausting shades of red. It
slays the hearts of men, beyond the hope of psychology! When you speak
the name of Tannis, you utter all that needs be  said!

# Little St. Simons Island

A Nature's Program Just One Channel Away!

An isle where Spanish moss hangs an extra length,
A place where you have always wanted to stay,
An island where wildlife thrives at full strength,
A nature's program just one channel away!

Unmarred, unmolested at the hands of man,
Maritime forests, marshes and wetlands lay,
Over 90 years still following the plan,
A nature's program just one channel away!

One hundred Snowy Egrets rise up and fly
Above the wetlands in the grandest display!
A Red-Tailed Hawk and Heron with fish sail high,
A nature's program just one channel away!

A ribbon of tidal creeks weave through marsh land.
The song and wading birds greet those from the bay
As sixty-nine Pelicans move in a band,
A nature's program just one channel away!

All four species of deer appear around bends,
So numerous, but each time brightening our day.
A fawn's mother, close by, tenderly attends,
A nature's program just one channel away!

A Berried Beauty Bush, Banana Spiders,
Indian Toothache Bark numbs pain the guides say.
The wonders never cease for this tour's riders,
A nature's program just one channel away!

To this show of nature's lavish excesses
Our safari enters with filtered sunray
The maritime forest deepest recesses,
A nature's program just one channel away!

Armadillos, alligators coexist,
All ten thousand acres of island portray
A balanced harmony of nature persists,
A nature's program just one channel away!

Perhaps, though, the highlight of this day's pleasures
Was seven miles of beaches that parlay
Unspoiled resources of sea shell treasures!
A nature's program just one channel away!

A staff of twenty professionals play host
To thirty so privileged that come here to stay,
To lodge and to feast on this gem off the coast!
A nature's program just one channel away!

So don't be controlled by the other "remote"
When you could experience all that I say.
At Hampton Point you cross this channel by boat,
Little St. Simons one channel away!

I asked my new friends in adventure what they thought,
"Primeval, fresh, wild, pristine, what a day!
An exotic solitude this island brought,"
Little St. Simons one channel away!

# When I First Met Marian

Could love's dormant feelings be awakened by one beautiful face?
And long months of negative emotions suddenly erase?
Could dark clouds of adversity give way once more to the sun?
Can melodies of birds return upon meeting this special one?

She has the aura of springtime's bloom and youth in her looks.
She supersedes the beauty and lure in all romantic books.
She calls herself old fashioned, she's well-bred and educated too,
She relishes her role as "Mom" as "50's" mothers would do.

Her sweet smile, her eyes, her features smite me without Cupid's aid!
And though I've been through betrayal and hurt, with her I'm not afraid.
A genuine personality who sparkles for all she meets.
She lights up St. Simons like our lighthouse to all she greets.

She trained in voice at a prestigious school in her resumé.
That's all I've learned of this sweet lady on our very first day.
Except, she is from Brunswick, storms drove her back to her home place.
A retreat home left by her kind father for this time to face.

She, too, has traveled through valleys and life's tumultuous seas,
Though, trial's cocoon may hem us in, in time its captive frees.
Her treasure is her daughter, and so, her daughter treasures her,
I consider them treasures too, for I'm drawn by her allure.

September 24th, 2000, the day we met by "chance."
And each time, hence, my first thoughts of her have only been
enhanced!

## Qui S'y Frotte S'y Pique,
## Mind Your Own Business!!

What do you think of the duBignons,
The French who made Jekyll their dominion?
Their coat of arms insinuation:
Qui s'y frotte s'y pique, Mind your own business!!

What made Christoff Poulain duBignon,
Take flight during the French Revolution?
Some foes wanted to serve his head with onions!!
Qui s'y frotte s'y pique, Mind your own business!!

While fleeing on ship he had a vision,
Of buying his very own island,
And running a private plantation.
Qui s'y frotte s'y pique, Mind your own business!!

Grandson, Henry Charles duBignon,
In the War Between the States division,
Endured houses, fields, burned by the Union!!
Qui s'y frotte s'y pique, Mind your oun business!!

And, then, his son, John Eugene duBignon,
He built a cottage with no plantation,
And sought to make friends with those with $millions.
Qui s'y frotte s'y pique, Mind your oun business!!

But despite this change of disposition,
His servants still whistled when bringing food on,
To keep them from nibbling his Filet Mignon!!
Qui s'y frotte s'y pique, Mind your oun business!!

A series of plans, then, were laid by John,
He bought the island for $13,000
And stocked it a hunting reservation.
Qui s'y frotte s'y pique, Mind your oun business!!

And, then, he invited those with $millions,
To hunt on his new reservation,
They hunted, then bought Jekyll Island!!
Qui s'y frotte s'y pique, Mind your oun business!!

They paid one hundred twenty-five thousand!!
They toasted the deal with Don Perignon,
With John smug he followed his intuition!!
Qui s'y frotte s'y pique, Mind your oun business!!

Take care what you do with this information,
You could start the next French Revolution!!
Why are you nosy about the duBignons?
Qui s'y frotte s'y pique, Mind your oun business!!

### *Pronunciation Keys:*

*("key-see-fraught-see-peek")*
*John and tion  -(Shawn)  gnon –(yawn)*
*(French Cajun Sounds)*

# Beautiful Beth and the Bard

Although running never was for me
Easy exercise–it's rather been hard,
Now that I run alongside the sea,
We are Beautiful Beth and the Bard.

Though country roads, once, were inviting,
Years I jogged past creeks and wooded yards.
Yet, I find the sea much more exciting!
We are Beautiful Beth and the Bard.

One day, off on my run to East Beach,
Quite suddenly, was I caught off guard
Matching strides with a sweet "Georgia Peach,"
We were Beautiful Beth and the Bard.

Talking came easily as our strides
As waves beside us rose up and sparred.
Our highs and lows we could confide,
We are Beautiful Beth and the Bard.

It takes two to enjoy such scenery!
Dophins splash as if our bodyguards,
Four feet from the edge of our sea!
We are Beautiful Beth and the Bard.

Moonlight waves her bright wand o'er the ocean,
Reflecting white sands–even night cannot mar.
Two joggers drink this magical potion!
We are Beautiful Beth and the Bard.

We know the sea has made note of us,
Entrusting us with such rich reward
As we run toward the sunset at dusk,
We are Beautiful Beth and the Bard!

# Constitution Oak

Constitution Oak so stately stands,
Once planted by Calvin Coolidge's hands?
Photographers caught him in the act,
The nation's media to attract!

But... he was given the wrong oak tree,
Switched, later, with no publicity!
Thus, may presidents cover their rear,
For they are not always as they appear!

## Were Our Laura To Be Showcased...

I tell you of a gorgeous sight
Blue eyes, brown hair, a perfect tan,
A semi-tropical delight
Too perfect for a mortal man.

How long can St. Simons conceal
A beauty so slender and tall,
A model, an actress reveal
And show her perfection to all?

The Barbie Doll is now replaced
And shown to be only a fad.
For, were our Laura to be showcased
An audience in wait would be glad.

For here's a beauty also smart
Her spontaneity is such fun!
The chances are she'll win your heart
Before a performance is done.

So world, so large beyond our shores
Make room for one of our own!
For all she needs is open doors
To let her true beauty be shown!

# The Cloister's Whippoorwill

The Cloister's Whippoorwill, quite undisclosed within the leafy oak,
Calls to none that could threaten, none that could hunt,
None that would reveal her hiding place.
To whom then does this shadow of secrecy call?
Not to the woodland's beasts, nor to the scurrying small,
Nor to other fowl whose talons and beaks could snatch,
Shake or tear.

To whom, then, but the shining sphere heralded above the earth.
Whose gentle beams of light warm, soften, snuggle and cheer
Even the darkest of night's creatures.
It is to this reflected source of happiness
To whom, even the Whippoorwill, must overcome shyness
And cry out as loudly as any of night's participants,
Her joy of partaking.

# Kirby

What can I say about Kirby?
A princess looking for her "frog."
But when I look at her features,
There's none that leave me in a fog!

She laughs and with her eyes as well,
In her an impish spirit dwells!
She "funs" the "mun" out of the mundane,
She rocks the heck out of the plain!

She entices with subtle charm.
She'd never do anyone harm.
She'll always be young and beautiful!
She's also sincere and "dutiful."

Every single day she's the same,
So here's to Kirby as a name!!

# One Sandcastle Vs. The Sea

The sandcastle stood resolutely on the seashore,
Oblivious to the encroaching, poaching, changes of tide.
For it was well-constructed by a family of four:
Two men with shovels, two ladies shaping four tiers with pride.

In two and one-half hours of fortifications grand,
Complete with look-out towers from which to view approaching waves.
Yet did this edifice know it was only made of sand
And when a sandcastle faces the ocean's force, it caves?

Hours later, scouting waves arrived to check out the moat,
Encircling, surrounding, even playfully, at first.
Then, reinforcements joined them, making the structure take note.
It was only then, the sandcastle began to fear the worst!

Then came a frontal attack upon the hours-old wall.
At first chipping, then ripping, troops assaulting from the rear.
The sandcastle stood as much as it could, and then began to fall!
As it was leveled at high tide, its architects stood near,

Proud that it had taken all of one-half hour to bring it down.
It was just one day's family vacation rendition,
With plans for one ev'n stronger as the builders gather round,
One to top the last, in their annual week-long tradition!

## A Lady Named Heather

There was a young lady named Heather
Desiring to blow off like a feather!
But, her husband named Joe, didn't want her to go,
And promised to love her forever.

So Heather is caught in cross breezes,
For were she to do what she pleases,
She could lose her true love, she thinks so much of
And nothing the pain of that eases!

When thoughts of this kind beset her,
That what is good could be better,
It could lead to a maze and waste many days,
And she may regret that he let her!

# She Is...

She is, I observe, one of the few ladies any single man would choose to have as his own. Not only is she a woman a man would love, she is a woman any man should love, for she has beauty quite unassumed, but very real in the natural.

Her hair is sandy blond and curly, creating a celestial knit and woven fabric of softness. Her face has the fairest traits and designs in all the earth, yet unabashedly borrows perfection from Heaven. Her eyes radiate a wholesomeness of spring's rich green meadows basking below the extended heights of mountain crests topped with still white snow. The gentle sloping of her cheeks are like rolling hills before those same mountains, yet, there is nothing too sharp or angular in her features.

Her loveliness does not drive men away as though unapproachable, but invites them to befriend her, as her gentleness makes only kinder even the most gentle of gentlemen. Her divinely sculptured forehead, nose and chin add to the warmth and allure of her exquisite portrait. A beauty she would be in any age, though not as a goddess who has business on earth, but as a real live inhabitant who cheers and encourages those in whose presence she finds herself.

Yet, this abundance of beauty, that from her very being and body emanate, is not reflected back into any sort of vain glory or self-absorption, but, rather, a sort of naiveté and sparkling genuineness. Her lips, when she speaks, makes men to feel blessed to hear sweet spoken words flowing through the most feminine and tender of her facial features.

Before leaving the dear subject of her face, I must also make mention of the light that through her expressions shine. Mostly sunny, but even on rare days when a hint or threat of clouds casts a shadow over her countenance, yet, never is her glory as a woman eclipsed!

I have not allowed my mind (as a man) to drift below her shoulders for there might I be tempted beyond my devoutest, most chivalrous and most sacred of intentions. For I am content to be this blessed creature's friend. As she endeavors to help others through thoughtfulness and occupational pursuits, I am determined to help her any way that I may.

And what is my reward? To rediscover these endearing traits in each of our meetings and to thank the God of Heaven that she, this wonderful she, is my friend!

Welcome to the real and imaginary world of artists' minds
To their observations and memories of various kinds
You'll discover magic comes as much from their
Souls as through their eyes,
Where canvases may be illustrated with
Recent or childhood ties.
Where portraits introduce you to people you have never met
See paintings, pottery, sculptures in most shades sunrise to sunset
And if nature's colors are dull, artists simply supply their own!
You must go to a gallery where such works of art are shown!
You will see how light affects objects and objects affect light!
Their passions rival my own.
Their talents surpass in their own right!!

## The Lifestyle Of Kim

There is a cute lady named Kim
Who's living her life on a whim.
The first thing detected–
She does the unexpected
For that is the lifestyle of Kim.

If ever she seems perturbing,
With you does something disturbing,
At least she's not boring,
She wakes up the snoring,
And that's worth a lot of "perturbing!!"

# Deborah Kate!

My Love, beautiful beyond fair words!
Your smile, bright above the sun's rays,
Your eyes are radiant like shimmering stars,
Your cheeks blush like Valentine bouquets.

Your eyelashes lure me with one blink,
Your hair, the softest sheen a man could caress!
Your chin, another unflawed feature,
Your lips invite impulses hard to repress!

A 1958 dance in Heaven,
To bright music of the seraphim,
A single note of joy escaping,
Began a chase by the cherubim!

"Perfection must be kept in Heaven,
Don't let this note of joy reach earth!
If it merged with the sun's golden rays
The celestial sun could give birth!"

The angels chased her to this world,
Arriving in the peak of the fall,
Where she landed safely upon a leaf-
The fall's most colorful one of all!

The joyful note, sun rays and the leaf,
That night were kissed by a shooting star!
Pursuing angels gave up the chase
As night breezes carried her afar.

Alighting on the back of a swan,
Which guided her to an obscure town.
A baby- then girl- then lady hiding,
Lest angels came back to look around.

Each night stars celebrate this secret
Which they keep from the angels above.
Yet, I, wishing upon that shooting star,
Was visited by this one I love!

So, Deborah Kate, I feel that fate
Has brought you from Heaven's portal!
I find in you Heaven's joyful note,
And the sun's golden rays immortal!

The leaf of fall's most brilliant color,
The shooting star, the nighttime breezes,
The elegant swan's graceful gliding,
Such beauty withheld only teases!

Do you now see what I say is true?
Although, you may not know what to say?
For that's why I can only love you,
And I have since our very first day!!

# McEvers Bayard Brown

A port though a haven between land and the sea,
Becomes a portal for adventure's liberty
From land's disillusionment and lost love's misery.
Could it become a chain from which you cannot break free?

A sad case was that of McEvers Bayard Brown.
He built a lovely cottage close to Jekyll Sound,
A young New York banker who joined Jekyll Island Club,
The home built for his love, but therein was the rub.

Although he had chosen a lovely bride to be
And it appeared the marriage was a certainty,
The home furnished, the wedding planned elegantly,
But, who knows a woman's heart with any certainty?

His fiancée left the island, never to return!
His love for her, however, never ceased to burn.
While living on board his yacht waiting for her change of mind,
His hopes like sand in an hourglass repined.

The cottage, secluded for romance with his bride,
Became where he allowed his servants to abide.
So, he languished on board his yacht, the Valfreyia.
'Til one day, all hope gone, he left America.

He set sail for England, to the Essex Coast,
Where he, a port-bound yachtsman chose to stay the most.
His crew of eighteen awaited orders to sail,
The yacht engines were in readiness so as not to fail.

But there, in that port, he grew old as a hermit.
The thought "there might be someone else," he'd never permit!
In that state existed until the day he died,
With orders to return him to where love was denied.

His heart tired of mourning the bride he still dreamed of,
They buried him in America, where he lost his love.
A chimney is all that remains of his dream home,
The visions of wife, children, never his to own.

A port though a haven between land and the sea,
Becomes a portal for adventure's liberty
From land's disillusionment and lost love's misery.
It could become a chain from which you cannot break free!

# Love Tides In!

# Your Dreamy Brown Eyes

How may pupils so small in your dreamy brown eyes
Contain a world so large that beckons me there!
I enter the world within your dreamy brown eyes
And find it pleasant to stay as long as I dare!

What rich beauty there is in your dreamy brown eyes,
A cascading and sparkling, pure stream of delight!
That I'm so mesmerized should come as no surprise,
All else around me is lost when you're in my sight!

I dream as I gaze in your dreamy brown eyes
Still hoping the love in your eyes was for me,
When, once, I saw love there in your dreamy brown eyes,
For eyes never shone with such intrigue and beauty!

And had you only beauty in your dreamy brown eyes
And were not your face graced with features most fair,
The loveliness within your dreamy brown eyes,
Alone, sets you apart as a beauty most rare!!

# Susan

Susan is a sunbeam,
The sun's brightest ray.
Susan is a sweet dream,
Who brightens even day.

Place her in the night sky
She would outshine stars!
No moon, nor moons need try,
Her light would reach Mars!

Her inner qualities
Charisma and charm
Blessed with rare quantities
Sweetness to disarm.

Angels in their splendor,
Next to her appear plain.
Her beauty's tender,
Like Tulips in the rain!

Susan! Night is not dark,
Day is not mundane,
Susan provides the spark,
Light through the window pane.

Her laughter, her smile,
Radiate from within her.
I make no denial,
I'd love to woo and win her!

Knights jousting to the death,
A small price for this prize!
I'd walk the kingdom's breadth,
I'd fall for no disguise!

Her beauty discovered
By all who meet her,
Royalty uncovered,
Loyalty, allure.

She'd be a fair creature,
Without this light within,
Heaven's love has graced her,
I've been graced since when,

My eyes were mesmerized
When our eyes first met!
My heart quickly surmised
She's sunrise and sunset!

# There's Something Different About This Play

A pleasing part of an actor's life is playing scenes
    romantic,
To kiss a beautiful lady as part of a scene fantastic.
I admit I've rather enjoyed this –creating an illusion,
But something's different about this play, I feel there's
    no delusion!

But masking my feelings for you, has taken a heavy toll,
For, since our first kiss in "Caesar," I haven't been
    playing a role!
When I looked in your playful eyes, as blue as nature's
    bluest sky,
And your big, bright, beautiful smile, I've never before
    soared this high!

Then when my lips first touched yours, so soft and
    tenderly inviting,
You replaced feelings long dormant with new ones
    much more exciting!
Niagara boasts no greater rush than I feel with you in
    my arms.
There may not be a remedy- I'm enchanted by all your
    charms!

If you agree our romantic scenes are more than just a
    teaser,
Then why can't we rehearse them still, long after
    Julius Caesar?

Co- written by Keith Johnson and Terry Herbert,
former brothers, Leonato and Antonio, in a production of Shakespeare's "Much Ado About Nothing."
Brothers for life, Terry helped Keith write this
poem about his love interest in another play. What
are brothers for??!

# Pictures Of Your Pretty Face

How lovely is beauty so shy
That does not its special wares flaunt!
From summer 'til now I did try,
Through fall's changing hues I did want

Some pictures of your pretty face,
An image of Nature's fairest child.
Five months could not our meeting erase,
Deep yearnings, each day, have compiled.

Then came a promise that you'd send
Your pictures by mail on Monday.
My prayer to Heaven did attend,
I received your pictures on Tuesday!

On Georgia's coastline I await
While, you live on the state's west side.
On June 9th, we had our first date.
Oh, why must Georgia be so wide!

By angel, fairies, I care not,
But, swift your pictures came to me.
I have in my hands what I sought,
I still delight in what I see!

Your cheekbones elevate your beauty
As mountains rise high above the plain.
As seekers treasure rare booty,
Your description defies my brain!

Your eyes so sparkling and tender,
Alluring warmth of color brown.
Like the autumn's burst of splendor,
You're a princess without a crown!

Your hair needs none with highlights soft
A brown reflecting golden rays,
Descending glory  returns aloft,
Like golden wheat during harvest days.

Some ladies have chiseled their noses,
Cosmetically, for perfection.
That they seek your traits presupposes,
You pass perfection's inspection!

The moon is beautiful round and full,
The quarter moon sleek and slender,
Esthetically, outshines the whole.
Your face, feminine and tender,

On my heart makes this  impression,
Is like two quarter moons combined,
An elegant fair expression
Of heavenly beauty refined!

A rainbow bends downward to gold—
The pot of gold at rainbow's end.
Your lips, were I to be so bold
One kiss, would I to Orion send!

I held your pictures for an hour,
And three were swiftly placed in frame.
As daffodil's your best loved flower,
My favorite lady bears your name!

# Pretty Deborah!

Pretty Deborah! Your name's like chimes in gentle breeze,
Pretty Deborah! Your name is long yet flows with ease.
It's like a stream winding down the mountainside,
It's like a carefree beach at lowest tide, Pretty Deborah!

Pretty Deborah! Your name inspires so much in me!
Pretty Deborah! You are the sand, the surf, the sea!
You're like Pansies showing through the snow,
You are diamonds wrapped up with a bow, Pretty Deborah!

Pretty Deborah!  How can I make you truly see?
Pretty Deborah!  You're like the breath of life to me!
You are daybreak's crimson bursts of light!
You are the moon's warm hues to cheer the night,
Pretty Deborah!

# My One Wish

As Autumn leaves scatter in the winds,
So time does distance us from our past.
Some fond, familiar faces it rescinds
As many of our friendships do not last.

Were I to be granted one single wish,
My dear, it would concern my love for you.
In my ocean, there is only one fish.
Where else would you find a love more true?

For beauty chooses the form of your face,
My heart treasures you  more than purest gold!
A bag of gems one might hold, not embrace,
Embracing you grants me riches untold!

The greatest blessings in life come freely,
Who could purchase the vibrant sun above?
I will treat you, fairest lady, genteelly.
For with my one wish, I'd wish for your love.

# Lord, Give Me A Lady
## Whose Hair Is Brown!

Now, ladies are a work of divine art,
So long as from God's scheme they seldom part!
Some feel there's something dull about hair that's brown.
Say, red would look stunning with an evening gown.
What they can't see in a mirror's reflection,
Is red's not the color for their complexion!
God makes redheads with skin to compliment,
That's fair or with freckles to be as He meant.
Some so-called "improvements" work to their harm,
As though brown is without its own set of charm!
What if the bluebird were sick of being blue,
And chose to dye herself with some color new?
There's nothing she could find not already in use.
The change might subject her to verbal abuse!
For all of nature leaves well enough alone,
And no creature looks for new colors or tone.
Yet, so many women think sexy is blond—
Not to say its something of which men are not fond.
But blondes possess the lightest and fairest of skin.
Becoming a "blonde" may not help you to win
A man who should love you just as you are,
Who's not looking to wed some Hollywood star.
For brown has a luster all to its own,
It shines with the prettiest shades men have known!
Dark hair and dark eyes truly accentuate
The prettiest features men appreciate!
Why did God make more with brown than other shades?
To dislike your hair's hue, the issue evades.
I'll shout it aloud to all within my voice's sound,
Lord, give me a lady whose hair is brown!

# Yours Is The Beauty

Yours is the beauty of the world's silv'ry oceans,
The lowlands' bluest lakes,
The highlands' loftiest peaks.

Yours is the freshness of spring roses,
Of rushing rapids, of fall's red maples,
Of winter's earliest snow.

Yours is the sparkle of a starlit night,
Of a mine's prize diamond,
Of the morning's first light,
Trumpeting its brilliance
And awakening the world!

Yours is the grace of a dove in flight,
Of a doe bounding through the forest,
Of a butterfly lilting above a lily.

Your voice and laughter draw me
Like a cat to a warm sunbeam upon the floor,
Like a bluebird to her nesting young,
Like a bee to its flower's nectar.

Your love distinguishes me from
All the other men of the world.
As Mt. Everest is the highest,
The Grand Canyon, the deepest,
The Pacific Ocean, the widest,
So your love overflows my heart,
Soul, mind, and body,
And crowns me a king among men!

# If Beauty
## Were A Nectar

If beauty were a nectar and
poured into a mould,
Alone and only ladies could
with promise yet untold,
To thus reveal the form of
Nature's fairest features,
With grace to take their place—the
World's most pleasing
Creatures!

And were they lined end to end,
a continent's length in all,
And were I to view them from
the petite to the tall,
And were I to walk that line to
search out beauty's best,
But, you would stop me and my
heart as fairer than the
Rest!!

## Are You A Painting?

Are you a a painting waiting for an artist's touch?
Would you look best Italian, Spanish, French or Dutch?
Are you a symphony that's yet to be composed?
Would you be in over'ture or concerto transposed?

Are you poetry's rhythms, eloquent yet terse?
Would you be a rhyme or would you be free verse?
Could your beauty inspire literature's best?
Would romantic tales of you diminish the rest?

Will you be the leading lady for all my plays?
Would you "steal" each performance with the most bouquets?
The answer to all of these is "yes" on my part,
For you are all of these and more in my heart!

# My Love Inspires Music

My Love inspires music,
from Heaven's inner portals
Which wafts down on sunbeams
to the ears of this world's mortals.
And though the songs she inspires
are like the snowflakes pure,
That they come to me through her,
she would rather find obscure.

My Love fills my world with magic,
yet believes not in the same,
Nor dreams of herself inspiring
the fairest rose's name.
My Love, with such care, adorns
herself in pretty dresses.
Yet does she know it's she, not clothes,
who draws my warm caresses?

She loves sunshine, yet knows not,
her face all the brighter shines!
She's fair, yet does not know,
she's fairest of all valentines!
I daily try to show her,
she's as special as all this,
While I have learned,
that her one sweet ignorance
is my bliss!

## What Happiness Is There!

What happiness is there,
like when we kiss and embrace?
My uneventful days,
you totally erase!
One glimpse of your face...
I live for each sighting!
And when we make eyes,
it's all too inviting!
And when we're alone,
day or evening is exciting!
And when we're apart,
I send love to you in writing.

You are the essence of life to me.
My life's enriched by your beauty!
You are the essence of love to me.
No man could call loving you duty!
Except I found love with you,
I would have searched endlessly for love.
'Less I grew weary looking below,
how found I this gift from above?
Who brings warmth to my winters
every time you call?
Who adds beauty to beauty each spring,
summer and fall?
Who but my lady, my friend,
my life, my love, my all!

# How Grand
# The Scope Of Beauty

How grand is the scope of beauty,
As vast as this wide world,
Where ladies of all nationalities,
As far as lands are hurled,
Possess their own unique features
That portray beauty best to their men.
Yet, doubtless, I find you most fair
Of all the places I've been!

# Dreams Of Desire

At first, you were a dream, like an angelic messenger by night. That dream planted the seeds of desire in my unsuspecting heart, which, when sown to the wind, scattered the meadow of my mind with flowers. From desire, arose opportunity, for only one needs seek it. When sought and found, it still takes two to complete it. For the two must engage to be engaged, to pleasure to be pleasured, a couple drawn by currents like that of the great tidal sea. At first, back and forth, but then a swirling current which holds each from drifting away, or like in the eye of the storm, a pocket of calm although disorder around them might reign!

A spring, so refreshing, enlivening, that it takes the strongest pull to separate them for their daily duties. But, nothing more than a void in time is needed to draw them quickly together again.

As all birds of flight must return to their roost, the eyes of each lover beholds the other as more special than themselves, and the giving of pleasure to the other becomes the source of all pleasure received. As the two in love grow into one, his world and hers are but few rotations apart. Together, then, buoyed by the force of love, they can realign the far flung galaxies, and fulfill earth's most cherished and happiest of summer days.

The momentum which they create is unified, like that of a single snowflake joined with its kind, becomes potent to unleash a mighty avalanche down the steep, sleeping mountainside.

Now, what if the lady were my love, my one and only true love? God has given me breath and voice to say to her alone, "I love you!" God gives me boldness to admit, "I need you. I want you!"

While, some men see a universe of women in the world in which they live, I see a universe in the woman I love. And if Heaven should show favor to bring you to me as my love, I should never presume to ask so great a favor again!

# Love's First Moonlight

Relax, sweet Darling, and enjoy
Forces, rushes of rare delights,
Of a thousand moonlit nights!
Love so strong and yet quite coy
Enchanting a girl and boy.

Once they become woman and man
Feelings deepen, grow and mature.
Yet, hurts may make them feel unsure.
If we've lost loves over a span
Those we chose disappoint Love's plan.

This time, though, Love has chosen us,
Revealing feelings long since lost,
Appreciation from the cost.
Unrequited love brings us thus,
Tender affections with no fuss!

Moonbeams gathering form a boat,
Our high mountain, valleys below,
There's nothing from our past to tow.
Our souls, now free, begin to float
Swirling waters around Love's moat.

This sturdy ship could take us far
Following streams down to the sea.
That is where you were brought to me!
Love's first moonlight is where we are,
Why not sail to the farthest star?!!

# Love's First Kiss

Love's first kiss...
More splendid than the day's first rays,
Than the night sky's first shooting star,
Than the outburst of spring's first days,
The tide rushing over the sandbar.

Love's first kiss...
With desires of hurricane force,
Ravishing like a twister's cloud,
Like a ship maintaining its course,
Or the roar of the jungle's proud.

Love's first kiss...
More heat than August afternoons,
More molten than the volcano's ash,
More passion than love's sultry tunes
Addicting like the gambler's cash.

Love's first kiss...
Tenderly became two, then four,
Then found the realm of ecstasy,
A dozen kisses at the door!
Now love is more than fantasy!

Love's first kiss...
Though prince and princess we are not
But, yet, fairy tales may come true,
For there appeared the love we sought
Only after I first kissed you!

# Love's First Bliss

I would not give my love away
Despite what ladies do or say,
Not if a lady meant nothing,
Not if a lady meant something –
Not even if she meant something!
But, when she means everything

The horses long corralled stampede
While I concentrate on her needs.
We're swept along a swelling bank,
Restraint's dam crumbled and then sank!
White water sweeps us to a ledge
And rushes us over the edge!

The thrill of acceleration,
The fill of exhilaration!
Before we fall we shoot to the moon,
In time for a lunar typhoon!
The stars leave their heavenly spheres
To dance with us 'til our course veers.

We skirt Venus' full ecstasies,
Reality of fantasies!
Exploding stars throughout the night,
Exploring feelings to their height,
And when we have experienced all
Embracing, still, we take a fall.

Tenderness, lovingness, at rest
We must now fall back to love's nest.
Though not the rush of the trip up,
We know we have drained passion's cup!
As magic loosens her powers,
We savor bliss for many hours!

# Passions and Breezes

The desires of my love,
are  for my Lady intended.
I am the stem, lifting my Flower,
fully extended,
So she may bask in the warmth
of nature's passions
And breezes,

While I'm impassioned to keep her there
as long as she pleases!
Where the sense of tender touch,
overrides the other four.
Where her moments do not quickly end,
but she begs yet for more!

My Love is like a rose blossom,
petals shaped to perfection!
Her eyes, hair, face, complexion,
are nature's perfect reflection!

As roses' folds accentuate
as you get near the center,
So my Lady's folds
are a swirl of delight where I enter!
As nectar within the blossom
attracts the scent of the bee,
So the sweet nectar of my Love,
arouses, entices me!!

# Love
# Tides
# Out!

# Cupid's Disclaimer

Poetic words take wings of flight–
The hearts of ladies, thoughts of men,
Exploring from the grandest height
Whatever takes place between them.

For all involved in love can fly,
Both Cupid and the fabled Zeus,
While Venus and her maids defy
Bold gravity's force with a truce.

If love has left your hopes forlorn,
Then, still, you tread upon the ground.
One kiss, and you could be airborne,
Emotions, passions, newly found!

Beware of Cupid's disclaimer
While reveling in love's rich mirth,
If your love is a complainer
You'll soon be crashing back to earth!!

# Singleness and Marriage

I've heard it said of men who like to "explore,"
For whom relationships are a revolving door,
That when they are single and would like to "mingle,"
The lovely girls are all tied down—the rest are a bore!

But if you tied down that same man in marriage,
As they leave the church in a horse-drawn carriage,
When he looks all around, single women abound!!
But now, he has a wife he must not disparage!!

# The Dawn Or Dusk Of Love?

The lustrous red hues of this redhead who I know,
I, somehow, mistook for the red of daybreak's glow.
I thought we would have an entire day to spend,
I felt we had much we could share before its end.
Petite, bright and fun, you are much younger than I.
Yet, when I looked again at the bright crimson sky,
'Twas not the birds of dawn opening number,
'Twas waning notes which they sing before they slumber.
Was I, the one, who confused the east and the west,
The stirring of the birds and the time when they rest?
You stirred my emotions, made my heart flutter!
When I responded, you started to sputter.
Much like winged fowl which are not grounded on earth,
Are flighty, skipping from branch to branch in their mirth,
Your mixed signals were the cause of my confusion.
As twilight hours hasten to their conclusion,
I'll walk on alone and count dark night my brother,
While, thus, to find a new sunrise with another.

## "What Lies Beneath The Snow"

I've loved you so long, how could it be wrong
For me to keep on caring?
You've been in my dreams forever it seems,
Our good and bad times sharing.

And what is so bad, the thoughts that I've had
That fairest are you of the fair?
To praise you for this in my marital bliss
Need not be a burden to bear.

Of garden delights, in discourse and sights
Make life with my lady appealing.
And who may pray tell, the depths of that well
Of her innermost thoughts revealing?

To realms unknown, but to me alone,
To heights of ecstacy reaching.
Beyond this world our love has whirled
My heart to yours beseeching.

Above this earth with little mirth
The mundane of each day.
With pain and grief without relief
Can love find a way to stay?

O what a cost when sight was lost
Of one great eagle soaring.
Cast we our eyes upon the flies,
Are not the insects boring?

But you and I were meant to fly
Our goals, ambitions gliding!
'Til we went down and thus were bound
Our hearts' true intents hiding.

Your dreams for us in the dry dust
You've left for Winter's hiding.
All covered by snow, the cruel winds blow
Yet hope of Spring abiding.

In hope for Spring and all it brings
Its scents and sounds abounding,
So here I wait-your garden's gate
For love's new life resounding.

At first a sprig and then a twig
And then the leaves are greening.
And then the dash of color's splash
Upon the flowers sheening!

How can you say that there's no way
Our love's exchange can grow?
When just a chance could greatly enhance
What lies beneath the snow!

# To My Departing Valentine?

From my imperfections to your love and defections
Happy Valentine's Day to you.
Could we still kiss on a day such as this,
Remembering when love was true?

But Cupid is grounded, his job now confounded,
Just when his arrows take aim,
He shoots for our hearts and finds but the parts
Of what was a whole now remain.

But still I'm a man who is following your plan
Locked in and while feeling locked out.
And yet when I look, you're the cover of a book,
Enough to make any man shout!

So why can't we try to bid by-gones goodbye?
Or waste all the vigors of youth.
Let's light both our fires with passion's desires,
Let ecstasy show us the truth!!!

# Love's Betrayal

I have only desires, no devices.
I think my virtues outnumber my vices.
Yet, you can look on me and pick out every flaw.
While, love could cause cold criticisms to thaw.

But since you turned from my love to find your own way,
There's nothing I could do to make you want to stay.
Were roles reversed, and were it I who wanted out,
How could I leave you without a lingering doubt?

I think our love has simply caught a summer's cold,
You feel it's fatal, together, we'll never grow old.
My feelings are pain, grief, disbelief, betrayal!
While, you feel nothing, at least that's your portrayal.

# A World Without You

Now my life is only filled with stems without roses,
Hives without honey, uncertainty a question poses.
I have clouds without assurance of a clear blue sky,
Nor sunshine, nor rainbow, nor winds to sweep my
storm clouds by.
I live in gardens without scents where ev'n flowers
appear drear. Since I live in a world without you and
your love, so dear.

# You Disappeared From My Mirror

My Love, you were such a beautiful love,
that I had to set a mirror above,
Above the bed where we played,
the bed where we stayed...
Long hours were like minutes with you,
l felt our love was perfect and true.
And suddenly, it all was past!
Who would have thought it would not last?
The love we made, the times we played,
...below my mirror.

My Love, the images your body brings!
The time when we had our flings!
Flings of your beauty and grace,
Flings of my passionate embrace!
The mirror shook with our emotion,
passion of two lovers in motion!

Lost to the world, our cares were free.
A whole universe with just you and me.
So how could such ecstacy end?
So you come you're barely my friend?
The love we made, the times we played,
...below my mirror.

You disappeared...You disappeared, from my mirror!

# The Quintessential Agonies Of Love

What quintessential agonies play out in love,
And even for lovers matched by Heaven above!
You felt death awaited you if you had to stay,
While painful deaths were my lot
if you went your way.
For you were a perfect loveliness in my sight,
And when your heart left mine,
my sunshine turned to night.
I died a thousand deaths in the darkest tomb,
yet, was I surprised, it was really a cocoon!
Once broken, I could sense the clearest
bright blue sky.
At once, I felt the impulse to rise up and fly!
So, I burst through the clouds where,
indeed, skies were blue,
And to my surprise I'd found my way  back to you.

# Farewell, Fair Mirage!

Farewell, Fair Mirage of my life!
I thought you were mine, I wed you
Never to know what's really true
About the lady, then my wife,
Only to learn from turmoil and strife!

You were a picture half-complete,
What I saw was beauty, indeed!
What I did not was never freed.
Rare times the other I would meet—
Momentarily, it was fleet.

Where there were gaps I would paint
Colors and shapes beautifully.
My love was yours dutifully.
My devotion never grew faint,
I thought you were nearly a saint!

That fateful spring of '99,
Finally, you dealt with your pain.
Dark clouds thundered with troubling rain,
Vats, full, emptied of bitter wine.
Then, I knew you were never mine.

Our marriage, a mirage, the whole,
Twenty-five years of history!
I held in my arms mystery,
Despite my intentions and goal,
Your body but never your soul!

## The Day You Took Off
## Your Wedding Ring

A ring, rounded, depicts eternity.
It shows how endless our love was meant to be.
Our vows were heard by friends and family,
The day we exchanged our wedding rings.

Four hundred witnessed our oaths of true love,
Which we made before God who dwells above.
We thought we would last like two turtle doves,
The day we exchanged our wedding rings.

A year from our silver anniversary,
Forgetting the good times, despondently,
You said, "It's over. I want to be free!"
The day you took off your wedding ring.

I asked you once more, again, to wear it,
Our 25th! I wanted us to share it.
But ev'n for that night, you could not bear it,
A year after you took off your wedding ring.

I tried in vain to woo you back to me,
A year and one-half devotedly.
All hope gone, I threw it into the sea,
The day I took off my wedding ring!

My ring lies beneath the ocean's wake,
Where yours lies is anyone's guess to make.
Was our love true, or were we a mistake,
When we put on and took off our wedding rings?

# It's Over!

I've felt my last heartache, I've dried my last tear.
You've put me through "hell" for six months and a year!
When you said, "It's over!," you nearly stopped my heart!
I felt my life was over, if we'd ever part!
I never knew such agony before in my life!
It hurt more than Mom and Dad's deaths to lose my wife!

I've tried a thousand ways to win you back to me,
I sought to woo you again with my poetry.
My voice irritated you, you did not want my touch,
You didn't want my company very much.
So now you want divorce, you never gave me a chance,
And I've wanted to give you everything with romance!

It's like you took pleasure in destroying each love's token,
My heart is wounded, but I haven't been broken.
I've run a thousand miles to burn off this stress,
I've hit the weights from the "curl" to the bench-press.
I've been immersed in prayers by friends I could talk to.
I've searched God's Book to make sense of your saying
"we're through!"

I even moved to an island, a walk from the beach,
You said "I'll give you a chance" here only to breach!
I've spent a fortune trying to win you back.
You gave me no credit, were quick to attack!
You hold me dearly accountable for this mess,
While I am flawed, my effort was my best.

As autumn leaves drop 'til there are none left to fall,
Our vows, our wedding rings mean nothing to you at all.
I now agree, "It's over!" sounds good to me too!
I'll have a new life with someone who remains true.
Though I'd not release myself from my wedding vows,
You've crossed the line my threshold of pain allows!

# A Golden Ring
# Flung Into The Sunset

A golden ring flung into the sunset,
From off The Pier, reflecting the sun's last rays.
A glorious gasp of when we first met,
Then, you became mine, the happiest of days!

The soaring sphere you once placed on my finger,
On the long awaited day we became one.
Ev'n when you changed, I wanted our time to linger,
Your love, though, was waning like the setting sun.

Now, night lies in wait for the chance to take over,
Destroying all the happy remnants of day.
A dark, enshrouding, villainous rover,
Which would not allow our "daylight" to stay.

A pink, you would love, hangs on the horizon—
A band of our dreams which have fleeted away!
Perhaps, it is the pallor of a poison,
Affecting your mind, suggesting what you say.

A silhouette of a bridge yet uncompleted,
(Were Sidney Lanier to write about this!)
Were not your emotions spent and depleted,
Could not we cross spans toward marital bliss?

But now these last images fade into night.
Is darkness and emptiness all that shall be?
My wedding ring, with no splash, sank out of sight,
A fitting ending, a burial at sea!

# A Golden Ring
## Flung Into The Sunset *(con't)*

But I cannot stay on this side of The Pier,
When, where I am gazing offers no hope.
I must turn my back on visages so drear.
In looking away, I may learn how to cope.

I went to the other side and there was amazed!
I had not been left in darkness alone,
For as I looked, I was no longer dazed,
For the beacon, "The Lighthouse," so brightly shone!

And besides this light supplied by man's care,
A guardian from shipwreck for those in distress,
I looked toward the sky and what found I there?
Not just the moon, the full moon, such brightness!

My life will go on, the best is in store,
But, never, I'll be without a guiding light!
And I may even romance and love once more,
For there are no wrongs God cannot make right!

# "It Isn't Christmas Yet"

A Memory From My Childhood Years
A Christmas Tree, A Boy In Tears,
A Mother Knelt To Calm His Fears,
  "It Isn't Christmas Yet."

"With Christmas Season Drawing Nigh,
Just What Could Make A Child Cry?
No Presents ' neath This Tree So High,
  "It Isn't Christmas Yet."

Now What If Christmas Came And Went,
And Not A Dime On Gifts Was Spent,
And Nothing Through The Mail Was Sent?
  "It Isn't Christmas Yet."

The Mother Wiped His Tears Away
And Drew Him Close So She Could Say,
"You'll Have Your Share On Christmas Day,"
  "It Isn't Christmas Yet."

The Small Boy Heard His Mother's Word,
His Joy Secured, His Hopes Endured.
His Fears Were Gone When She Assured,
  "It Isn't Christmas Yet."

That Scene So Real Is With Me Still.
As Is That Christmas Morning Thrill!
Her Words Were True, I Had My Fill,
  "It Wasn't Christmas Yet."

A Lesson Learned Should Not Be Spurned
As Years Flew By My Thoughts Returned,
To Hear Her Words Once More I've Yearned
"It Isn't Christmas Yet."

I Know My Heavenly Father's Love
In Ruling , Guiding From Above,
In Life's Great Storms, What I've Thought Of,
"It  Isn't Christmas Yet."

"O Perfect Love," Our Hymnal Rhymes.
How Could Such Love Send Trying Times?
The Answer Rings From Steeple Chimes,
"It Isn't Christmas Yet."

The God Of Grace I Have Implored
Though Oft It Seems I've Been Ignored.
I'm Prone To Doubt My Loving Lord.
"It Isn't Christmas Yet."

"My God Shall Supply All Your Need."
Perform This Verse, Lord, Which I Read.
I Wish You Worked At Greater Speed,
"It Isn't Christmas Yet."


Now Trials Come In Seasons Too.
We Cannot Stop Them 'til They're Through.
Lord, Make Me Faithful Make Me True.
"It Isn't Christmas Yet."

My Faith Though Pure, May Be Quite Small
And He Who Thinks He Stands May Fall,
So May I Conquer, Endure All.
"It Isn't Christmas Yet."

No More From Trials Will I Shirk.
"Let Patience Have Her Perfect Work,"
No Matter What Ahead May Lurk,
"It Isn't Christmas Yet."

My Dreams Were Dashed While Others Dance
But Hopes Aren't Left To Circumstance.
Give God's Calendar One More Glance,
"It Isn't Christmas Yet."

Now, Christmas In A Soul Set Free
Brings Love, Joy, Peace, Prosperity.
In God's Own Time We All Shall See,
"It Wasn't Christmas Yet."

Open Your Windows, Lord, And Pour
Your Gifts Of Grace From Heaven's Store.
We'll Shout On Earth And Heaven's Shore,
"It Wasn't Christmas Yet."

# Love, Lost And Found

As a romantic, I must acknowledge
ladies as most fair,
From their toes to the various colors
and lengths of their hair.
For I may dutifully gauge what
I still feel at this stage--
Say fifty~ that by their lovely gender
and actions tender,
They send electricity, magic,
and fragrance through the air!!

Now were I a realist,
I would readily admit to you,
That not always are outward beauties
matched with inner graces too.
(What I thought was forever,
a quarter century did sever!!)
But despite the pain I deeply feel,
I must hold to the ideal,
For what's lost could be restored,
meeting that special, someone new!!

# Epilogue

Shall I choose an epilogue to end this? If it flows like the ocean's tides, perhaps. If not, it were better ended a page ago.

The Golden Isles are, truly, a semi-tropical paradise of the rising and setting sun, the rising and lowering tides. A place where sweet love is born, nurtured, consummated and rekindled on anniversaries. A place where others may go to nurse love's loss amidst the balm of an island's separation and serenity.

Had I the beauty and words of Shakespeare's Rosalind, my epilogue would charge those in love to embrace and hold their embrace through all the storms and changing tides and times of life.

I would charge others, whose eyes daily search the ocean's horizon for a new ship and a true love, to never allow the beacon light of their hopes to become extinguished.

I would charge those whose love has been shipwrecked beyond repair to allow the sea to sink and settle that wreckage out of sight and out of mind. If necessary, as I have done, they may choose to throw a token of that lost love into the sea from the sunset side of the Pier on St. Simons Island. Then, one day, it may be their happy lot to follow my lead once more, on "The Lighthouse" side of The Pier, where I shall propose marriage to my new love.

The complete work, *Love Tides and Golden Isles Lore* is available in a 3-CD collection.

The poems are recited by the author, Terry Herbert, enhanced with ocean and other sound effects and mood matching guitar introductions by recording artist, Tim Haynes. [100 min.]

Send $24.95 plus $4.00 S/H
Check or money order to:
Terry Herbert
P.O. Box 24588
St. Simons Island, GA 31522

A special lover's gift edition of the *Love Tides In* CD is also available. The poems are recited by author Terry Herbert with mood matching guitar introductions by recording artist, Tim Haynes. [30 min.] Send $12.95 plus $4.00 S/H to above address. This same CD with a Valentine cover may be ordered one month before and through Valentine's Day at no extra charge.